YOSEMITE

A Picture Book to Remember Her by

CRESCENT BOOKS
NEW YORK

Books Ltd., Guildford
in Barcelona, Spain by
A
tion published by Crescent Books, dist   wn Publishers, Inc.
ISBN 0 517 61403 0
a

It was in 1851 that the first journalists and writers found their way into Yosemite Valley. The sight that met their eyes staggered the senses. Cliffs so high and granite mountains so huge they amazed even the most hardened explorers; giant Sequoia trees so old they defied any known means of measuring time; waterfalls that seemed to come from the sky and plunge into eternity; and a wilderness so vast and remote that to this day man has not seen it all. At first, its sheer beauty and grandeur caught their imagination and, through their reports, the imagination of the rest of the country. Gradually, however, people who visited the valley became more and more aware of the necessity of preserving this miraculous discovery for future generations. This concern resulted, in 1864, in the midst of the Civil War, in President Abraham Lincoln signing an act giving Yosemite Valley and the Mariposa Grove of big trees to California "to be held for public use, resort, and recreation, inalienable for all time." Thus was established the first state park and the beginnings of the national park movement.

People from all over the world who can now share the beauties and wonders of the national parks owe a great debt of gratitude to one man in particular: John Muir. Born in Scotland and raised in Wisconsin, Muir was a writer and naturalist who influenced generations of conservationists and can justly be credited with siring national parks.

John Muir went into Yosemite in 1868 and became obsessed with what he saw. He campaigned for years to make a national park of the Sierras and their meadows surrounding Yosemite Valley. His writing had considerable influence, and in 1890 his dream came true: sixteen years later California re-ceded the valley and the big trees to the federal government. It was whole at last.

To say, simply, that Yosemite Valley is beautiful beyond decription is an understatement. The place moves everyone, without exception, and no-one leaves without having been touched by it in some way, even if only by the immensity of it all.

El Capitan, the largest block of granite on earth, defies even the wildest imagination, as do Half Dome, Glacier Point, and other mammoth peaks and pinnacles. They can at first seem frightening: should they come crashing down in some cataclysmic earthquake, it would seem the world would end. Yet when we walk among them for a while they seem to become giant guardians of the fragile life in the valley below.

"These sacred mountain temples are the holiest ground that the heart of man has consecrated," wrote Muir "and it behooves us all faithfully to do our part in seeing that our wild mountain parks are passed on unspoiled to those who come after us, for they are national properties to which every man has a right and an interest."

John Muir was a prophet: Yosemite had been his beacon. Those who read his words and see his land blessed with the "holy spirit of light" can never forget.

Dep. Leg. B-12.680-87

Facing page: Nevada Fall.

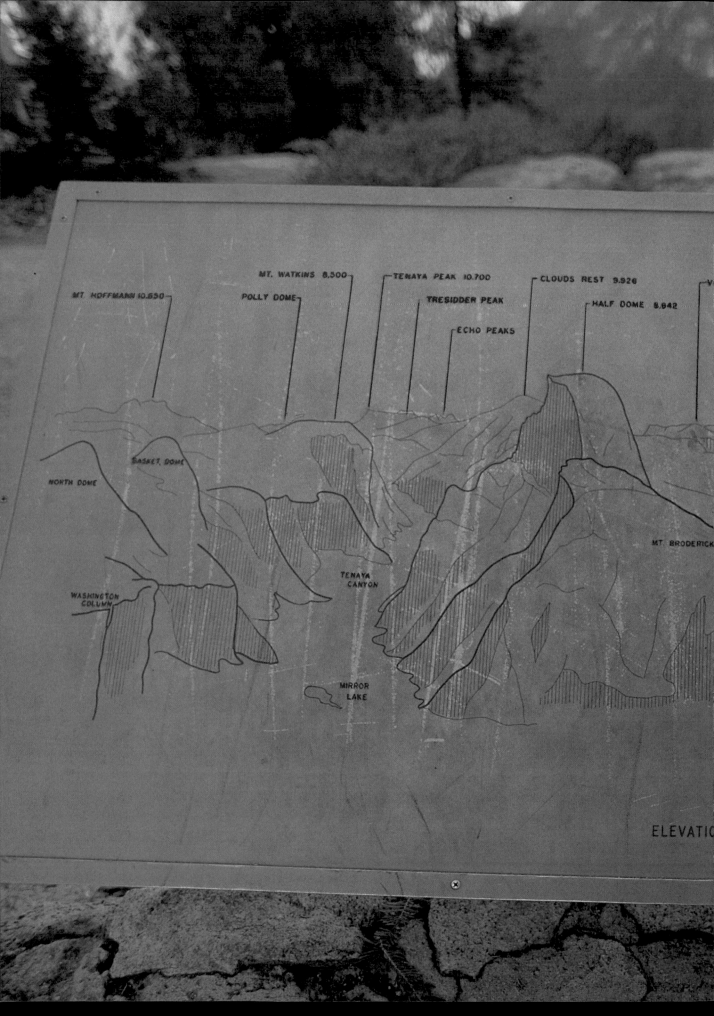

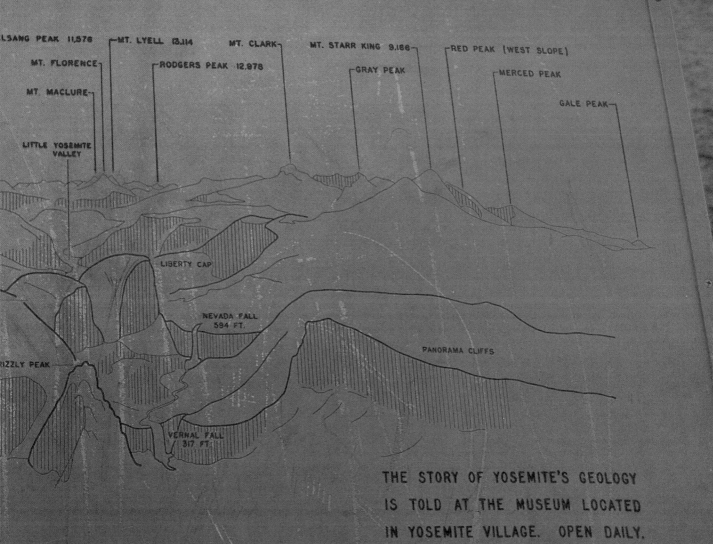

LSANG PEAK 11,576   MT. LYELL 13,114   MT. CLARK   MT. STARR KING 9,166   RED PEAK (WEST SLOPE)

MT. FLORENCE   RODGERS PEAK 12,978   GRAY PEAK   MERCED PEAK

MT. MACLURE   GALE PEAK

LITTLE YOSEMITE
VALLEY

LIBERTY CAP

NEVADA FALL
594 FT.

PANORAMA CLIFFS

RIZZLY PEAK

VERNAL FALL
317 FT.

THE STORY OF YOSEMITE'S GEOLOGY
IS TOLD AT THE MUSEUM LOCATED
IN YOSEMITE VILLAGE. OPEN DAILY.

— 7,214

Previous pages: a map at Glacier Point, naming the major peaks of the Yosemite Valley and illustrating the breathtaking extent of the view from this lofty platform. These pages: the 739-meter cascade of the beautiful Yosemite Falls, the highest waterfall in North America. Overleaf: the valley seen from Tunnel View, with the mighty bulk of El Capitan on the left, facing wooded Cathedral Rocks.

Previous pages: (left) a creek by Route 140, and (right) Half Dome, glowing in the evening sun. Top: Dewey Point, (above) woodland near Half Dome, and (right) sheer rocks near the Lower Yosemite Falls (top right). Facing page: Bridalveil Fall with Cathedral Rocks and (overleaf) with Dewey Point.

Previous pages: (left) golden leaves and (right) a
shallow river in the Yosemite Valley. Among the most
awe-inspiring of Yosemite's natural wonders are the
giant sequoia trees, the largest of all living things.
They are to be found towering over pine trees in the
forest of Wawona (above), an Indian word allegedly
meaning "big tree" and, more profusely, in Mariposa
Grove (facing page), the largest of the park's three
main sequoia groves. Overleaf: (left) Valley Chapel,
near Yosemite Lodge, and (right) Bridalveil Fall.

Previous pages: lush vegetation and great, gray boulders in the Mirror Lake area. Right: a Jeffrey pine on top of Sentinel Dome, gnarled and twisted over the centuries by fierce storms. Remaining pictures: examples of the rich diversity of the park's vegetation, which includes the soft, silky waterside grass (above) near Phono Bridge, and the bright green bracken obscuring the floor of Yosemite Valley (facing page). Overleaf: Yosemite Falls, seen from Tunnel View.

The Ahwahnee Hotel (previous pages left), one of Yosemite's best-loved inns, was built in 1927 from local granite and offers spectacular views of the surrounding scenery. Previous pages right and facing page top: Half Dome looming above the golden foliage of early autumn, and (top) dominating the view from Glacier Point. Above: looking west from the Yosemite Falls Trail and (facing page bottom) a tributary of the Merced River reflecting El Capitan and Cathedral Rocks. Overleaf: the delicate pastel shades of Yosemite Valley, once called the "incomparable valley."

Previous pages: Tenaya Lake (left bottom), one of the largest of the park's lakes, was named for the chief of the Ahwahneechee Indians, a tribe who lived in the Yosemite Valley for centuries. (Left top) a tributary of the Merced River near El Capitan, and (right) a view from Olmsted Point, near Tenaya Lake. Above: looking from Taft Point towards El Capitan, (top) visitors enjoying the view from Glacier Point, 975 meters above the valley floor, and (facing page) Grizzly Peak, seen from the Mist Trail near Vernal Fall. Overleaf: (left) El Capitan, and (right) Cathedral Rocks.

Previous pages: the Merced River dropping over 181-meter Nevada Fall, with the snow-capped peaks of the High Sierra beyond. Above and overleaf right: the last rays of the sun shed a strange golden light on Half Dome. It was such magical light effects that led John Muir, one of the earliest explorers of the area, to describe it as a "vast celestial city, not clothed with light but wholly composed of it." Right: Siesta Lake seen from Tioga Road, a scenic highway passing through the beautiful high country and Tuolumne Meadows, north of Yosemite Valley. Facing page: (top) Nevada Fall, seen from the John Muir Trail, and (bottom) Half Dome reflected in Mirror Lake. Overleaf left: Cathedral Rocks, half-obscured by late-autumn mists, overlooks the Merced River.

Previous pages: aptly-named Mirror Lake, which unfortunately is silting up and within years will become a meadow. Facing page bottom: 2,695-meter-high Half Dome, the sheer north face of which was once covered in granite slabs that were peeled away by glaciers during the Ice Age, and (remaining pictures) conifers and shady trees by the Merced River, near Yosemite Lodge. Overleaf: the waters of the Merced River tumble over the 98-meter drop of Vernal Fall.

Previous pages: the verdant, forested floor and rose-tinted peaks of the Yosemite Valley at sunset. A different look is brought by winter, which lends a near-monochrome beauty to the valley and veils the snow-dusted forms of El Capitan (above) and Cathedral Spires (facing page) with wisps of light cloud. Overleaf: (left) Vernal Fall, and (right) strange calcified rocks, called tufa, rising from ancient Mono Lake, which lies east of Yosemite National Park.

Previous pages: Nevada Fall. Top and final page:
sequoias in Wawona Grove, and (right) in Mariposa
Grove, the site of the Grizzly Giant (above and
facing page), which, at 2,700 years old, is thought to
be the world's oldest sequoia. Overleaf: the
Yosemite Valley seen from Tunnel View.